# Contents

Introduction .................................................................. 2

## SEGMENT ONE: OURSELVES

| Episode 1 | How Do I See Myself? | 4 |
| Episode 2 | Who Am I Really? | 6 |
| Episode 3 | Who Can I Become? | 8 |

## SEGMENT TWO: OUR GOD

| Episode 4 | How Do I See God? | 10 |
| Episode 5 | Is God My Father? | 12 |
| Episode 6 | What Did Jesus Do for Me? | 14 |
| Feature | Soul Health | 16 |
| Episode 7 | Can God Live in Me? | 18 |
| Episode 8 | Can God Use Me? | 20 |

## SEGMENT THREE: OUR WORLD

| Episode 9 | What Happens at Home? | 22 |
| Episode 10 | What Happens at Work? | 24 |
| Episode 11 | What Happens at Church? | 26 |
| Episode 12 | What Happens with My Enemies? | 28 |
| Episode 13 | How Far Does This Go? | 30 |
| Daily Bible Readings | | 32 |

**FAITH CAFÉ EDITORS**: Kristi Cain, Laura Derico | **WRITER**: Chris Maxwell | **DVD VIDEO PRODUCERS**: Charles Powell and Gary Moon

Faith Café is a registered trademark of LifeSprings Resources and is used with permission. Licensed adaptation Copyright © 2007 Standard Publishing. All rights reserved. Published by Standard Publishing, Cincinnati, Ohio. Printed in USA. Scripture, unless otherwise indicated, taken from the HOLY BIBLE, NEW INTERNATIONAL VERSION®. Copyright © 1973, 1978, 1984 International Bible Society. Used by permission of Zondervan. All rights reserved. Scriptures marked *The Message* taken from *The Message*. Copyright © 1993, 1994, 1995, 1996, 2000, 2001, 2002. Used by permission of NavPress Publishing Group. When passages are paraphrased by the editor for the sake of clarity, they are consistent with a commitment to the verbal, plenary inspiration of the Bible. Cover photo © Tim Pannell/Corbis. Interior photos from Dreamstime.com: p. 2 © Zoom-zoom, p. 4 © Ioana Grecu, p. 6 © Luba V Nel, p. 8 © Fabrizio Argonauta, p. 10 © Celso Pupo rodrigues, p. 12 © Henry Fu, p. 14 © Xyno, p. 16 © Starfotograf, p. 18 © Stanislav Mikhalev, p. 20 © Wendy Kaveney, p. 22 © Stanislav Mikhalev, p. 24 © Alexey Averiyanov, p. 26 © Elena Kouptsova-vasic, p. 28 © Emin Ozkan, p. 30 © H3ct02, p. 32 © Boguslaw Kupisinski; from BigStockPhoto.com: p. 3 © Dirk Paessler. All Web site addresses were accurate at the time of printing. Any corrections can be sent to Standard Publishing, www.standardpub.com.

# Introduction

Peek in the window of your local coffeehouse. A few people sit with friends; others sit alone. Some listen and others laugh. People talk of weather, business, politics, and the friend who didn't make it there. Conversation goes in many directions, as varied and rich as the shades of coffee beans in the jars that line the wall. Customers come to drink coffee, to relax, to get recharged—but mainly they come together for community.

Many of us are ready to sit together and talk about life—real life, not just the weather or the latest sports scores. To offer you an opportunity to join in the discussion and probe deeper, we welcome you to Faith Café. More than a class and more than a sermon, Faith Café is a place for exploring truth and experiencing eternal change.

We start by studying ourselves: not self-help sessions, but investigations of our own self-views. In these first three episodes we ask, "How Do I See Myself?" "Who Am I Really?" and "Who Can I Become?" Probing Genesis and the Psalms, critiquing excuses, and daring ourselves to face our real lives, we offer opportunities to understand what living on this planet is really about.

The next segment of five episodes turns the attention toward the one who made us what we are and can make us more than we thought we could become. Who is that? You guessed it—God. To better understand God, we've allowed biblical texts, common statistics, and personal stories to lead us toward meaningful answers about him. We also pose some questions too many of us think, but refuse to voice: "How Do I See God?" "Is God My Father?" and "Can God Use Me?"

Moving from ourselves to our God leaves us one place to conclude for the final five episodes: Our World. Again, we find answers by identifying the questions: "What Happens at Home?" "What Happens at Work?" "What Happens at Church?" "What Happens with My Enemies?" and "How Far Does This Go?" These final episodes answer in more detail the earlier question about whether God uses us, and the answer is yes!

## ENTER

In our gatherings we do not want you just to sit back and listen. Faith Café invites you to enter into an environment where it is safe to ask for and seek answers. Phrases lure your mind toward deeper paths; quotes dare you to stare into your real self; questions give you a chance to talk to yourself and your friends about what is relevant in your lives.

Introduction | 3

## DRINK

This segment highlights portions of Scripture to help you gain a better understanding of truth, while friends beside you voice their own reflections about how the biblical story inspires them to believe in new ways. Your soul can be refreshed by drinking in the living water of God's Word.

## SAVOR

You will savor the stories of the struggles, musings, and triumphs of imperfect people like us who are journeying into a deeper relationship with Jesus. You will get a taste of ancient reality as it touches our fast-paced culture. And these bites of life will help to guide, challenge, and focus you.

## EXPERIENCE

Faith Café also offers statistics to investigate, books to read, video clips to watch, Web sites to peruse, and thoughts to ponder. The discussions of our society today will provoke groups to enter and experience lessons together. You'll create community and in doing so, learn more about yourself.

## WALK

As we examine society's trends and scrutinize Christianity's core beliefs, we choose not to leave it there. We offer suggestions to walk out with the truth you've explored and straightforward strategies for declaring doctrine daily to those around you. Actions such as writing letters, serving meals, or visiting hospitals will allow you to take your faith and share the delight with desperate people.

Every session includes an invitation to experience the truth you're studying on a regular basis. Spiritual disciplines such as intercession, silence, worship, study, and journaling help move you toward transformation. Your heavenly Father can guide and change you as you evaluate your habits and lifestyle.

You are invited to taste and see, to drink and be refreshed. By reflecting and exploring, by examining and investigating, by meditating and applying, you just might discover a way to know God more and to get closer to the person he created you to be. We have no doubt you'll be glad you decided to sit, sip, and talk about life at Faith Café.

# EPISODE 1 | OURSELVES

# How Do I See Myself?

## ENTER

Are you feeling as if God is way off in the distance? Or maybe you're not sure where you are in your relationship with him?

Welcome God to the "café" of your inner life . . . that place where the real you lives, where the creature God made lives, where hurts and hopes and anger and joy all merge.

Offer this request: *God, as I seek to learn more about myself and about you, I ask you to forgive me of my mistakes and welcome me into your café. Thanks.*

These café conversations are about living life—about not just believing that a real spiritual experience is possible, but helping it happen. Enter the café and relax, breathe, look around. You never know what you'll find there. Today you might find you.

---

It's time to place an order at the Faith Café. Order your inner desires. No one is going to see this except you and God. As you think through the menu in your mind, ask yourself these questions:

- What do I hide about myself?
- What words would describe how I see myself and my relationship with God right now?
- Who do I wish I could become?
- What words do I wish described me?
- Is that order, or request, possible in my life right now? If not, why not? If so, how?

### Consider it

"They cannot parody you unless they know you, and when they know you, it means you're part of the culture, and when you're part of the culture, it means you're successful."

—Joan Rivers, from an interview in *The Week*

## DRINK

*Oh, oh, oh . . . How empty the city,*
*once teeming with people.*
*A widow, this city,*
*once in the front rank of nations,*
*once queen of the ball,*
*she's now a drudge in the kitchen.*
*She cries herself to sleep each night,*
*tears soaking her pillow.*
*No one's left among her lovers*
*to sit and hold her hand.*
*Her friends have all dumped her.*
—Lamentations 1:1, 2 (*The Message*)

Lamentations is a book in the Bible that depicts the Jewish nation as a widow—a sad, lonely, defeated widow. Formerly ranked at the top, the nation had fallen to the bottom. Think of hurricanes or fires ruining neighborhoods and cities. Think of terrorist attacks changing a world. The Israelites must have felt destroyed, defeated, unwelcome anywhere and by anyone. They wondered if even God wanted them anymore.

Do you ever feel as if you are at the bottom? History helps us remember that Israel did not have to remain there. They were God's chosen people—set apart by God to be his own. To be loved.

4 | FAITH CAFÉ

As you trek through your own journey, you can join Israel in noticing what you think of yourself and what you should do to move forward. And you can remember that you don't have to stay where you are. You too are God's own. You are loved by God.

## SAVOR

Betty listened. She appreciated the speaker's honesty about the value of relationships. At one point, her mind wandered. His words about loving others lured her thoughts in a new direction. She questioned whether she had ever really loved anyone. Betty remembered the facial expression of a friend and asked herself, *What did I do to make her so angry?* She recalled the departure of a spouse and said, *Why did I blow it?* She realized that she isn't very close to many people and thought, *I can't blame them; I wouldn't be around myself if I didn't have to.*

Compare Betty's thoughts with these: "I'm so grateful to Christ Jesus for making me adequate to do this work. . . . The only credentials I brought to it were invective and witch hunts and arrogance. But I was treated mercifully because I didn't know what I was doing—didn't know who I was doing it against! Grace mixed with faith and love poured over me and into me. And all because of Jesus.

"Here's a word you can take to heart and depend on: Jesus Christ came into the world to save sinners. I'm proof—Public Sinner Number One—of someone who could never have made it apart from sheer mercy" (1 Timothy 1:12-19, *The Message*).

## EXPERIENCE

Comedian Joan Rivers has had bags removed from under her eyes, two complete face-lifts, cheek implants, fat injections, brow smoothing, teeth capping, neck tightening, a tummy tuck, and a nose thinning. She is quoted as saying, "When you look better, you are treated differently. People want to be around attractive people" (from "The New and Improved Rivers," *The Week*, July 15, 2005).

Does changing your outward appearance ever make you feel better inside? Why or why not? What does the approval of others mean to you?

### Look into it
- Psalm 8
- David Gregory, *Dinner With a Perfect Stranger: An Invitation Worth Considering*
- www.dinnerwithaperfectstranger.com
- www.perfectstrangemovie.com

## WALK

Do you want to move from sadness in yourself to acceptance of yourself? Do you really want to stop lamenting and start rejoicing? Then realize God's love.

This doesn't mean that you have to just sweep away your doubts or your negative self-talk. Admit and confess your inner struggle. But be willing to "take out" the truth you've learned today. As you might say in a real café, "I'll get this to go!"

"God loves you so much he wants what is best for you. He also wants to know if you want what is best for yourself."
—Stephen Arterburn, *Healing Is a Choice*

Carry a mug of God's love with you as you go through your week:
- E-mail someone who feels alone. Serve that person the meal of encouragement.
- Call someone you know isn't home. Leave a short message on the answering machine and try to encourage that person with your words and tone so he or she feels accepted.
- Stare at yourself in the mirror. Tell yourself God loves you. Repeat the phrase seven times.

**This week's spiritual discipline is journaling:** Write about any obstacle that is currently dragging you down or maybe hurting your relationship with God. Write your own lament. Then think about who you want to become and who God has created you to become. Write about it.

# EPISODE 2 | OURSELVES

# Who Am I Really?

## ENTER

"I am afraid to show you who I really am, you might not like it—and that's all I got."
—Sabrina Ward Harrison

In the last episode we talked about our self-views. Understanding how we see ourselves is crucial to becoming even better than we are. It's like making sure we know where we are on the map before taking the next turn. Today we continue the journey of investigating our lives as we digest the amazing taste of the truth. But before your next sip of coffee, ask yourself, "What do I really think about myself? How does that compare to what God thinks?"

Begin moving toward an opportunity to change who you think you are, and then change who you hope to become.

"Whose approval do you crave? Have there been times when you have sought the applause of men over the approval of God? How did you feel afterwards?"
—Mark Atteberry, *The Climb of Your Life*

Take a moment to look in a mirror. As you look at yourself from various angles, think about these questions:

- What do you like about what you see?
- What do you not like?
- How would you describe the person in the mirror to others?
- How much do you think your outer image resembles the person you are on the inside?

## Consider it

"Fact: It takes about twenty positive statements about ourselves . . . to counteract just one negative personal statement!"
—Heidi J. Raynor, ed. by Dr. C. River Smith, "Negative Self-Talk and Your Self-Esteem"
(© 1998 allaboutcounseling.com)

## DRINK

*God said, "Let us make man in our image, in our likeness, and let them rule over the fish of the sea and the birds of the air, over the livestock, over all the earth, and over all the creatures that move along the ground."*

*So God created man in his own image,*
*in the image of God he created him;*
*male and female he created them.*

*God blessed them and said to them, "Be fruitful and increase in number; fill the earth and subdue it. Rule over the fish of the sea and the birds of the air and over every living creature that moves on the ground."*

*Then God said, "I give you every seed-bearing plant on the face of the whole earth and every tree that has fruit with seed in it. They will be yours for food. And to all the beasts of the earth and all the birds of the air and all the creatures that move on the ground—everything that has the breath of life in it—I give every green plant for food." And it was so.*

*God saw all that he had made, and it was very good. And there was evening, and there was morning—the sixth day.*
—Genesis 1:26-31

## SAVOR

The man told Chuck, "You look just like your mama." Chuck smiled, nodding in kindness to a distant relative he hadn't seen in years. He laughed inside because a few minutes before, another person had said, "I feel like I'm looking at your dad whenever I see you."

Chuck had heard it all before: whom he looks like, talks like, and acts like. Instead of being bothered by the comparisons, Chuck chose to do his own self-evaluation. He grabbed his Palm device and wrote these questions before any more aunts or uncles could offer their critiques:

1. What do people think when they see me?
2. What do I think about myself?
3. Who am I really?
4. How does God view me?
5. How can I truly believe I'm made in the image of God?

## EXPERIENCE

Q: What is self-esteem?
A: Self-esteem is our internal feelings and evaluation of ourselves based on our perceived self-image.

Self-esteem and self-image are closely interrelated and are largely based on our feedback while growing up ([from] parents, peers, other important figures).

Fact: It takes about twenty positive statements about ourselves (the foundation of our self-image/self-esteem) to counteract just one negative personal statement!

Here's the difficult part: It doesn't take a continual repetition of negative statements from our parents, peers, and others throughout our childhood to cause low self-image/self-esteem.... Once we get a couple in our head, we can use them over and over again. Again and again, we take those false negatives and repeat them unconsciously (completely unaware). It's like having a constant heckler with you.

Can counseling help? Most definitely.... We need to replace negative self-talk with positive self-talk that we're willing to let ourselves accept. You can't draw on a chalkboard if there's an eraser following close behind. [Negative self-talk] erases the good, and replenishes it with bad.

—above taken from Heidi J. Raynor, ed. by Dr. C. River Smith, "Negative Self-Talk and Your Self-Esteem" (© 1998 allaboutcounseling.com)

### Look into it
- Psalm 139
- Timothy Jones, *Awake My Soul: Practical Spirituality for Busy People*
- Dr. Larry Crabb, *Understanding People*

## WALK

What did you learn from the mirror? from the story of how God created us? from Chuck's story? from Larry Crabb (in the video clip)? from the article on negative self-talk and self-esteem?

Let what you learned strengthen you to work and serve throughout your week. If you are a little timid about reaching out, read this:

"If you wait until you're really sure, you'll never take off the training wheels."

—Cynthia Copeland Lewis

Look into a mirror again. Choose to view yourself in a new way. Let today's truth change how you see that reflection—that handsome/beautiful, created-in-God's-image you!

- Think of a person toward whom you feel a little jealousy. Pray for him or her every day this week. Pray blessings, peace, and joy for that person, who is made in the image of God.
- Visit a local hospital, retirement center, or elderly persons' development. Remind those you see how God sees them.

**This week's spiritual discipline is silence:** Take time to be still, to think, and to hear the sound of silence. Work through the discomfort and find comfort with yourself.

# EPISODE 3 | OURSELVES

# Who Can I Become?

## ENTER

If we believe God made us, why do we let so much other junk invade our thoughts and feelings? Why can't we focus on the honor and privilege of being made by the all-knowing God? He made us. He really made us. And he is still at work in our lives, reshaping us with his care.

Take some time to reflect on these thoughts.

"We cannot become what we need to be by remaining what we are."

—Max De Pree

"Everybody thinks of changing humanity, and nobody thinks of changing himself."

—Leo Tolstoy

The way we hope to "become what we need to be" and change humanity by changing ourselves depends on believing these facts:
- I was made in the image of God.
- I have spiritual gifts.
- I am called for such a time as this.
- I am influencing the world.

**Consider it**
"Being able to label your gift(s) is not of utmost importance. Using your gift(s) is."
—from the Ministry Tools Resource Center, http://MinTools.com

## DRINK

*Oh yes, you shaped me first inside, then out;*
*you formed me in my mother's womb.*
*I thank you, High God—you're breathtaking!*
*Body and soul, I am marvelously made!*
*I worship in adoration—what a creation!*
*You know me inside and out,*
*you know every bone in my body;*
*You know exactly how I was made, bit by bit,*
*how I was sculpted from nothing into something.*
*Like an open book, you watched me grow from conception to birth;*
*all the stages of my life were spread out before you,*
*The days of my life all prepared*
*before I'd even lived one day.*

—Psalm 139:13-16 (*The Message*)

## SAVOR

Do we really want to recognize our strengths and build on them while admitting our weaknesses and finding help? Moving forward, instead of moving out, works.

I asked a friend how he moved forward, learning to walk again after a car accident. He said, "I worked and refused to stop until I walked. Then every morning I would wake up and have to force myself to walk again."

I asked a lady who had battled an eating disorder since her teen years how she moved forward. She said, "I focused on my positives and worked to improve them. I also confessed my weaknesses with total honesty and asked others to help me. If my friends had never confronted me to find help, I might not have changed."

I asked an alcoholic how he faced his addiction

8 | FAITH CAFÉ

and won the battle. He said, "I had to admit what I was really like. For too long I claimed not to have any problems. It helped me when I finally got help. Three times a day I voice my vows and pleas to God in prayer. Now, four years and seven months since my last drink, I keep moving forward one step at a time."

I asked a lady if she still struggles to forgive her husband for his affair. She said, "Remember when you told me to walk through the house and read the Scriptures loudly? Things have been better since then. I know it was more than that. The counseling, the prayers, the forgiveness, and knowing he is now held accountable. But it is like something happened in the house, or maybe in my spirit, that gave me hope again. I keep hearing you say that I need to remember how God also has forgiven me. Looking back, I'm so glad I didn't just run from the situation—or murder him—like I wanted to."

I asked a friend in prison what she would say to those of us who are still living in freedom. She said, "Stop wasting time. Don't make stupid decisions. Trust me, you don't want to end up here. But I also worry about those people who keep doing things that will never get them into prison. Their habits keep them locked in a different kind of prison. I'll tell you this, I am more free here—even though I hate it—than I was living that life of drugs."

Before I ended my visit in the federal prison, I asked the young lady to pray for me. Her honesty took reverence to another level. She didn't play a game. She pleaded to a listening Rescuer. Her prayer motivated me to stop wasting time.

(from Chris Maxwell, *Changing My Mind: A Journey of Disability and Joy*)

## EXPERIENCE

Think of this quote from *Changing My Mind*: "Moving forward, instead of moving out, works." Why do so many of us choose to "move out," to escape or avoid who we are and doubt who we can ever become? Wouldn't we be better off "moving forward"—finding our true selves and stepping toward accomplishment? What could make that more likely for you?

### Look into it
- www.christianet.com/bible/spiritualgiftstest.htm
- www.christianet.com/bible/personalitytests.htm
- www.mintools.com/gifts3.htm
- www.mintools.com/spiritual-gifts-test.htm
- www.advisorteam.org/the_four-temperaments
- www.keirsey.com/matrix.html
- www.personalitypage.com/four-temps.html
- Stephen Arterburn, *Healing Is a Choice*

## WALK

"Reduce the human job description down to one phrase, and this is it: Reflect God's glory."
—Max Lucado, *It's Not About Me*

If you think about that job description, how are we doing? What is our potential? How can we reach it?

Put a picture or other reminder of Jesus near your mirror. Realize that you are created to represent him. That is not adding pressure to condemn you. Rather than living under judgment, we can accept this realization as an honor and live it out in the hurried tasks of everyday life. Let's do it!

Take today's lesson to someone.

"I'm telling the solemn truth: Whenever you did one of these things to someone overlooked or ignored, that was me—you did it to me."
—Matthew 25:40 (The Message)

**This week's spiritual discipline is solitude:** To be in solitude means to hide away, to be alone, to reflect calmly upon ourselves and our lives. Take time to exit your normal rush, your common crowded and covered world. Rather than hiding away to escape problems, we can hide away with God, giving him our time. The private silence and stillness alone with God allow us to observe him and remember how he observes us—his creation. Enter the world of solitude and truly believe you are wonderfully made by God.

# EPISODE 4 | OUR GOD

# How Do I See God?

## ENTER

To move forward, it is best to know where we already are. We sometimes get glimpses of the state of our faith in unexpected places, such as while we're on a trip or when we're working on our finances. Understanding our spiritual condition can help us grow. In order to improve our relationship with God, we must also sometimes critique and confess our present view of God.

We have spent a few weeks finding out more about ourselves, but is that where we stop? Is that all there is?

Pray: *God, as we pursue a better knowledge of you and a relationship with you, help us grasp how we view you now. Lure us away from what is wrong, and dare us to dive into the truth of who you are.*

"True, God made everything beautiful in itself and in its time—but he's left us in the dark, so we can never know what God is up to, whether he's coming or going."

—Ecclesiastes 3:11 (*The Message*)

*A relationship with God.*

- How do you feel when you hear those words?
- What thoughts or images come to your mind?
- What memories and fears invade as you think of having a true relationship with God?

### Consider it

"When Christians say that they have faith in God, what do they mean? Do they know what they mean? Do they even mean anything at all?"
—Austin Cline, "Faith in God, Faith in Mumbo Jumbo" (http://atheism.about.com)

## DRINK

*Surely, O God, you have worn me out;*
 *you have devastated my entire household.*
 *You have bound me—and it has become a witness;*
 *my gauntness rises up and testifies against me.*
 *God assails me and tears me in his anger*
 *and gnashes his teeth at me;*
 *my opponent fastens on me his piercing eyes.*
 *Men open their mouths to jeer at me;*
 *they strike my cheek in scorn*
 *and unite together against me.*
 *God has turned me over to evil men*
 *and thrown me into the clutches of the wicked.*
 *All was well with me, but he shattered me;*
 *he seized me by the neck and crushed me.*
 *He has made me his target;*
 *his archers surround me.*
 *Without pity, he pierces my kidneys*
 *and spills my gall on the ground.*
 *Again and again he bursts upon me;*
 *he rushes at me like a warrior.*

*I have sewed sackcloth over my skin*
 *and buried my brow in the dust.*
 *My face is red with weeping,*
 *deep shadows ring my eyes;*

*yet my hands have been free of violence
and my prayer is pure.*

*O earth, do not cover my blood;
may my cry never be laid to rest!
Even now my witness is in heaven;
my advocate is on high.
My intercessor is my friend
as my eyes pour out tears to God;
on behalf of a man he pleads with God
as a man pleads for his friend.*

—Job 16:7-21

## SAVOR

Tim and Marie Kuck spent a Christmas in the hospital with their son Nathaniel. It was his first Christmas. They watched doctors and nurses and machines as the six-month-old child struggled to survive. As they suffered, Tim and Marie also heard their heavenly Father guide them to find ways of helping others deal with seasonal battles of sickness and sadness.

For the next three years the Kucks and many friends carried Nathaniel back to the hospital on Christmas to sing, smile, offer gifts, and pray for patients and their families. Through Nathaniel's multiple birth anomalies, surgeries, therapies, feeding tubes, and special care, the Kucks learned so much about how life really counts. Since four-year-old Nathaniel's passing to heaven on November 13, 2001, the Kucks have continued their holiday celebration of healing. Their ministry, Nathaniel's Hope (http://www.nathanielshope.org/), seeks to help families and friends realize those with disabilities really count.

(from Chris Maxwell, *Changing My Mind*)

## EXPERIENCE

"The good news is the Pursuer doesn't give up and keeps after us."

—Cecil Murphey, *The Relentless God*

During the next week, write a few sentences comparing your beliefs to those found in the Web sites below. If you have your own site, describe your view of God there. If you do not have a site, e-mail a friend from this group a description of your beliefs in God.

### Look into it

- Why many do not believe: http://atheism.about.com/od/doesgodexist/
- Why to believe: http://www.christianitytoday.com/cl/2000/002/6.36.html
- http://www.peterkreeft.com/audio/08_arguments-for-god.htm
- Gary Moon, *Falling for God*
- N. T. Wright, *Simply Christian*

## WALK

There are many times in our lives when our faith in God will be challenged. Learning how others view God can remind us of and challenge us to define what we believe, why we believe it, and how we can successfully live the truth in everyday life.

"Always be prepared to give an answer to everyone who asks you to give the reason for the hope that you have."

—1 Peter 3:15

Find out others' views on a supreme being.

- Spend time with someone you don't know very well. Ask that person if he or she believes in a higher power. Have the person describe his or her views of God.

**This week's spiritual discipline is reading:** We often choose to read small portions of Scripture, perhaps to save ourselves more time for staring at the thrilling pages of an exciting novel or a dramatic tale told on a TV screen. But the Bible contains stories of conflict, confrontation, drama, and discovery. This week's discipline gives us a chance to avoid letting our opinions control our decisions: make a choice to read the book of Job. Notice the honesty; observe the confusion; stay in the story. The discipline of reading through Job inspires us to endure whatever we face in life.

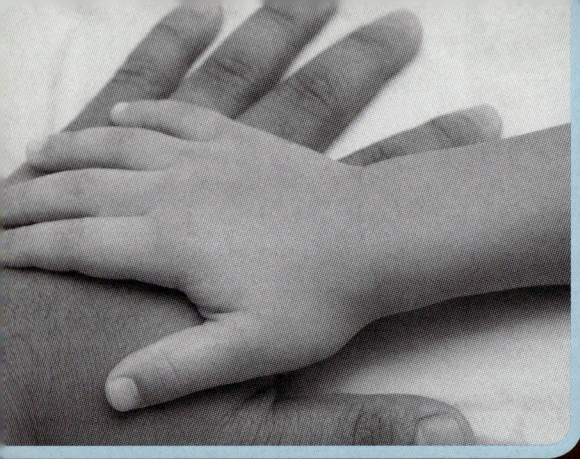

**EPISODE 5 | OUR GOD**

# Is God My Father?

## ENTER

Who we are and what experiences we have lived through shape our relationship to God. Maybe you have an easy time thinking of God as your Father. Maybe this concept is foreign to you, or even anxiety-producing. Take this opportunity to reexamine this facet of your relationship with your creator.

"You can tell for sure that you are now fully adopted as his own children because God sent the Spirit of his Son into our lives crying out, 'Papa! Father!' Doesn't that privilege of intimate conversation with God make it plain that you are not a slave, but a child? And if you are a child, you're also an heir, with complete access to the inheritance."
—Galatians 4:6, 7 (*The Message*)

Spend a few moments quietly reflecting on the following questions:

- *Daddy. Heavenly Father. Almighty God.* Which name for God are you most comfortable with? Why?
- Do you believe in God? If so, how would you describe him?
- How does God compare to your earthly father?
- What is God telling you to do?
- What has God done to you when you disobeyed?
- Are you willing to change your view of God if it is not correct?

### Consider it

"They expect that as a Father, he will respond to humanity, his children, acting in our best interests, even punishing those who misbehave like a father punishes his children, to restore those who trust in his love."
—from Wikipedia

## DRINK

*Grace and peace to you from God our Father and the Lord Jesus Christ. Praise be to the God and Father of our Lord Jesus Christ, who has blessed us in the heavenly realms with every spiritual blessing in Christ.*

*I keep asking that the God of our Lord Jesus Christ, the glorious Father, may give you the Spirit of wisdom and revelation, so that you may know him better.*

*Through him we both have access to the Father by one Spirit.*

*For this reason I kneel before the Father.*

*[There is] one God and Father of all, who is over all and through all and in all.*

*Sing and make music in your heart to the Lord, always giving thanks to God the Father for everything, in the name of our Lord Jesus Christ.*

*Peace to the brothers, and love with faith from God the Father and the Lord Jesus Christ.*
—Ephesians 1:2, 3, 17; 2:18; 3:14; 4:6; 5:20; 6:23

## SAVOR

Most of us choose to admire some things and people more than others. Admiring God can mean respecting and holding a high regard for him. But would it shock you to know that he also admires you?

*A personal reflection*

As I was waiting in the Lord's presence, he spoke this to me: "I admire you." This, of course, made me very uncomfortable as I wrestled with this obviously being a product of my flesh. But then he clarified what he meant by a picture in my mind. He showed me a picture of a young father standing over a newborn baby's bassinet, looking at the child with eyes of admiration that only a father can understand. Then I began to understand he admires us because he is a Father, and we are his children. That baby didn't do anything to deserve the father's admiration. As a matter of fact, all he would be doing is making smelly diapers, spitting up food given so lovingly, etc. Yet the father loves, admires, and takes care of him anyway! It was truly an encouraging word in such times of unknown future as these.

(Greg Amos, Christian education leader, Lake City, South Carolina)

## EXPERIENCE

Belief in God is higher in the Midwest (82%) and in the South (82%) than in the East (75%) and the West (75%). It tends to increase with age from 71% of those aged 25 to 29 to more than 80% for the three age groups of people over 40, including 83% of those aged 65 and over.

Women are more likely than men to believe (84% versus 73%). African Americans (91%) are more likely than Hispanics (81%) and whites (78%) to believe in God. Republicans (87%) are more likely to believe than Democrats (78%) and Independents (75%). Those with no college education (82%) are more likely to believe in God than those with postgraduate education (73%).

Church attendance (every month or more often) is higher in the Midwest (45%) and the South (40%) than in the East (30%) and the West (27%). It is lowest among people aged 25 to 29 (24%) and highest among those aged 65 and over (43%). And it is higher among women (41%) than among men (31%).

### Look into it
- For more information on this survey, please go to http://www.harrisinteractive.com/harris_poll/index.asp?PID=408
- http://en.wikipedia.org/wiki/God_the_Father
- Curt Cloninger, "Finding a God Who Is Big Enough" (Session One), *God Views*, LifeSprings Resources, 2003
- James R. Lucas, *Knowing the Unknowable God*
- Max Lucado, *Just in Case You Ever Wonder*

## WALK

"Dear Father, I have often become so busy in the details of my daily living that I have missed the joy of the love relationship you want to have with me. Open my mind and heart to discover the truths you want me to know. Reveal your love to me so that I understand and experience it in new and greater ways. Speak to me, dear Holy Spirit. I am listening."

—Steve McVey, *A Divine Invitation*

Try these ways of living out and sharing the truth of knowing God as your Father.

- Write a note to your heavenly Father. Offer him honest thoughts, feelings, appreciation, and requests.
- Then write a letter to a friend about God's love and acceptance. Use passages of Scripture to stay on the right track. Instead of signing your name, let your friend see it as a note to him or her from God's Word about his love.

**This week's spiritual discipline is worship:** Plan in advance to set aside at least ten minutes each day for only worshiping God: not in a church service or group setting, but you and God alone. Think about who he is. Do not worship the worship or let songs be at the center of your heart. Let God be. Enter a time of intimate worship of your creator.

EPISODE 6 | OUR GOD

# What Did Jesus Do for Me?

## ENTER

Jesus prayed, "I have given them the glory that you gave me, that they may be one as we are one: I in them and you in me. May they be brought to complete unity to let the world know that you sent me and have loved them even as you have loved me" (John 17:23, 24). In order for us to be clear about our relationship with God, we have to consider who Jesus is and what he has done for us.

"Neediness is a spiritual necessity. The whole point of the gospel is that we can't save ourselves!"
—Lisa Harper, *Relentless Love*

"Only one person could fill the bill, and the miracle of the cross is that he did."
—Rebecca Manley Pippert, *Hope Has Its Reasons*

> Some people may think about Jesus every day. Some may only think about him twice a year, if at all.
> - When do you think of Jesus most?
> - What do you think of when you hear the word *holiday*?
> - What images first come to your mind as you think about Easter and Christmas?
> - *Birth, ministry, miracles, death, burial, resurrection.* What parts of the story of Jesus' life hold the most meaning for you?

### Consider it
"Almost every viewer of this movie had a very strong opinion before they laid eyes on it."
—Danny Minton, on *The Passion of the Christ*, KBTV-NBC Beaumont, Texas

## DRINK

*They nailed him up at nine o'clock in the morning.*
—Mark 15:25 (*The Message*)

For God so loved the world that he gave his one and only Son, that whoever believes in him shall not perish but have eternal life.
—John 3:16

## SAVOR

A group of eager youngsters converge on a playground for an after-school game of baseball. Chuck, the tallest, is in charge. . . . The competitors ready themselves with warm-up tosses and exaggerated challenges. Chuck summons the group after brief moments of preparation, informing them that he and Wilson, as usual, are the captains who will choose teams. The group has endured the process frequently. The talented, or the most popular, get picked first. The awkward hopefuls experience the humiliation of being chosen last. If at all. That's how it is for Allen.

He is overweight and uncoordinated. His thick glasses and hand-me-down clothes provide ample ammunition for taunting from the insecure peers who never ignore such a perfect target. His name is Allen. Rarely do the boys call him Allen, opting instead for jests that attack his weight, his eyesight,

14 | FAITH CAFÉ

his clothing, or his clumsiness. So, on this day, he expects the usual round of ridicule as he suffers through the endless few minutes of rejection.

Allen, aware of his limitations, desperately longs for an opportunity, for a chance, for a friend.

Chuck chooses first. He always does. The eager candidates can easily predict the order of selection. Chuck regularly orchestrates the process to guarantee himself the upper hand. And to ensure that Wilson gets stuck with Allen.

Today, however, is different. Chuck looks relaxed. He doesn't hurry. He looks over the group several times, smiling as if he knows something they do not. Then, he shocks them all. He picks Allen. He picks Allen *first*. Not a good hitter, a good pitcher, or a good comedian. Allen. As other boys snicker, Chuck says, "I'm serious." Then he says, "Come on, Allen, I want you on my team."

Oh, the beauty of fairy tales. Underdogs win. Frogs become princes.

The story of our after-school ballplayers may not happen in our neighborhoods, but we would love for it to. . . . In the Gospels of Grace, we catch a glimpse of our dreams of glory. We see that fairy tales can come true. Jesus, this historical world shaker, claimed to espouse as his mission the releasing of the imprisoned and the loving of the unloved. He walked into the playground of the ancient eastern world and chose players for his team. His choices shocked those chosen, and baffled those observing in the stands of tradition and political correctness.

The gospel teaches, in a sense, that he has drafted each of us. Though we stand back, awkward and amazed, he hands us the bat. Though we're frogs, he kisses us. Though we're ugly stepchildren, he makes the slipper somehow fit.

He came, and comes, to give life to the lifeless.

(from Chris Maxwell, *Beggars Can Be Chosen*)

## EXPERIENCE

Read the Apostles' Creed:
*I believe in God the Father Almighty, maker of Heaven and earth, and in Jesus Christ his only Son, our Lord who was conceived by the Holy Spirit, born of the virgin Mary, suffered under Pontius Pilate, was crucified, dead, and buried. He descended into hell. The third day he rose again from the dead. He ascended into Heaven and sits at the right hand of God the Father Almighty, from whence he shall come to judge the quick and the dead. I believe in the Holy Spirit, the holy catholic [universal] church, the communion of saints, the forgiveness of sins, the resurrection of the body, and life everlasting. Amen.*

### Look into it
- Walter Wangerin Jr., *The Book of God*
- *The Passion of the Christ*, 20th Century Fox, 2004
- *The Visual Bible: The Gospel of John*, 2003

## WALK

Every day our attention is drawn to a thousand things. Most of us would probably have to admit that we spend too little time thinking about Jesus. But if we want to understand him more, that's exactly what we need to do—spend time with Jesus.

How can we help one another think of Christmas and Easter at unexpected times?
- Ask God whom in your group you could encourage this week.
- Consider sending a fellow participant a Christmas card or an Easter basket, just to remind him or her about Jesus.

**This week's spiritual discipline is meditation:** Prepare daily for the next time you receive Communion by slowly reading and rereading John 3:16: Meditate on the death of Christ and the command to remember his death until he returns. Allow each phrase of that verse to flood your mind and heart. Consider replacing the phrase "the world" with your own name. For example, "God so loved *John* that he gave his one and only Son. . . ." Finish this time of Christian meditation by thanking God for his great and overflowing love.

# Soul Health

## You can't be fruitful if you neglect the soul

### by Mindy Caliguire

Yesterday, I stood in front of a ministry team and asked, "What tends to emerge in the life of a person who neglects his or her soul? What symptoms creep in?"

I explained that no one ever sets out to trash the condition of his soul. Yet we often find ourselves in a spiritual death spiral. But we march dutifully onward, assuming that our spiritual state, a neglected soul, is somehow part of the "deal."

So I asked, "What are the signs of soul neglect?" At first the room was silent. Then somebody ventured, "Anxiety," and I knew they got it (not every group does). Once started, their answers came so fast I couldn't write them on the flip chart fast enough. "Self-absorption," they called out, along with "shame," "apathy," "toxic anger," "chronic fatigue," "lack of confidence," "isolation," "sin looks more appealing," "no compassion," "self-oriented," "drivenness," "loss of vision," and "no desire for God." Soon every inch of the page was crammed.

A sad feeling hovered over the room as these leaders saw themselves in the mirror.

Then, with much relief, we turned the page, and I asked, "What emerges in your life when you're deeply connected with God, when your soul is healthy?"

This page also filled up quickly: "love," "joy," "compassion," "giving and receiving grace," "generosity of spirit," "peace" (at this point, some bright bulb usually suggests the entire list of the fruit of the Spirit!), "ability to trust," and "discernment."

Heads nodded in acknowledgment as individuals recalled times when this was their experience too. All in all, a pretty desirable list.

Then I brought it to a vote. Holding up the Soul Neglect list, I asked, "Who votes for this?" Everyone laughed! No one in his right mind would choose to live this way. Then I called their bluff. "The truth is, you vote for one or the other of these two lists every minute of every day." Ouch.

The truth is, even Christian leaders can neglect the care of their own souls in their attempt to care for the souls of others.

Personally, I've known what it means to fail in this area. I crashed through every symptom of soul neglect when working with a team to launch a new church near Boston. Eventually my soul demanded to be heard. I was attempting to do everything in my own strength. Finally I heard the gentle voice of the Shepherd ask, *"Mindy, what part of 'nothing' (in John 15:5) don't you understand?"*

My soul's recovery was a slow one. Thankfully, I had a few soul-guides who led me into a new way of life that keeps me much clearer on my need for authentic connection to God. So my role at Willow Creek now is to highlight our intense conviction about the centrality of the soul and the urgency to find a way of life that keeps the soul healthy. The "how" of soul health is all about cultivating connection and receptivity to God, and that generally takes the form of spiritual practices that open the human soul to God. Woven together, these practices become a way of life that keeps the soul healthy. But living this way does require a fundamental shift, not just a better plan to be more organized or more "spiritual."

Most Christian leaders would agree that certain practices help us "grow." Prayer and Bible study make the top of almost any list. But given the current symptoms, it would appear that more is needed.

In addition to the role of Scripture and self-examination, these four practices are emphasized in our church's efforts towards spiritual formation in leaders.

## SPIRITUAL FRIENDSHIP

Spiritual friendship is the intentional pursuit of friends who help you remain open to God. Spiritual friends help each other pay attention to where God is at work in their lives and help each other respond.

Christians often live lonely lives of pretending. Sometimes, they're aware of the pretending; sometimes even they themselves are fooled. Spiritual friendship takes the "everything is together" mask off in very specific, human, in-the-moment ways. It's considered a "practice" because this vulnerability requires a willingness to enter the risky realm of being known as a person in process.

Tobias told me, "I approached friendships exactly as I was advised in seminary: 'Do not befriend anyone in your congregation.'" He had been instructed, "They need to look up to you; they need to see your example, and if you share your struggles, it will undermine your role as their leader."

He continued, "After a painful burnout, it finally dawned on me . . . we're telling ourselves that in order to be effective in ministry, we have to live a lie." Alone.

Admittedly, dangers lurk on the path to authentic relationships. But will we continue to live a lonely lie, or will we navigate these dangers for the hope of life, freedom, and transformation? That hope is well founded. But it will take a concerted effort, and practice, to build a spiritual friendship.

## CENTERING PRAYER

In working with groups, I'm often amazed at two things: first, how few enjoy a vibrant experience of prayer; second, how many Christians carry tremendous guilt about their lack of prayer. A double whammy! No wonder we don't like to talk about prayer.

Nonetheless, great healing and fueling power is released from God to us in prayer.

In this form of prayer, there are no more words, no more agendas, no more striving. This is an open, surrendered, peaceful way of resting in the presence of God. Centering prayer is not an absenting of the soul, as in Eastern mysticism, but being very much present with God. It requires practice and patience as your soul learns to become quiet.

Try centering prayer for about twenty minutes once a day for a week. Be prepared for the onslaught of ideas and images that will invade. No matter, you can gently release them and return to the quietness of soul (100 times per minute if your mind is like mine was when I started!). As my friend Lynne told me, "God loves your intent to be attentive, even if your attentiveness wavers with embarrassing frequency."

Over time, you can say, like the psalmist, "But I have stilled and quieted my soul" (Psalm 131:2).

## SOLITUDE

This is time alone with God. Why is solitude so potent? Because it frees you for a while from many things that would otherwise drive you. We can be invisibly driven by our egos, our fears, our insecurities, or even other people. Solitude helps us recognize and confront voices other than the Holy Spirit's.

Solitude also protects those unique parts of you that will get lost along the way if not guarded. What is that for you? Do you know what's at stake? Artists might say, "I lose my creativity." Elders say, "I lose my discernment." Leaders may say, "I lose clarity of vision."

Note what Jesus did. After a "run" of demanding ministry commitments, "very early in the morning, while it was still dark, Jesus left the house and went off to a solitary place."

In solitude he regained clarity. It fueled his unflinching resolve. Who today doesn't need clarity amid clamoring voices? Who doesn't need inner resolve to set and keep a direction? We all do. We need times of solitude.

## SIMPLICITY

In the wake of the current secular buzz around simplicity, it's important to be clear about what simplicity is and isn't from a biblical perspective. If you were to adopt the view of *RealSimple* magazine, for example, you'd see simplicity as intentional efforts to reduce complexity in your life, to make life more manageable. As nice as that sounds, it's not what we are after.

For a follower of Christ, the enemy of simplicity is not complexity. It's duplicity. Double-mindedness. The apostle Paul hardly led a complexity-free life. But he led a life of deep integrity and focus. That's the simplicity we seek.

Overbooking my schedule is a deeper spiritual issue than merely managing my life's complexities. At its core, it's me being dishonest about who I am and what my limits are. It is an insistence upon self-rule, not upon God's calling.

Simplicity rests on single-mindedness: letting your yes be yes; your no, no. Simplicity is bringing one's whole self into union with God's purposes: every dimension, every thought, and every decision under the direction of God.

I ask individuals to explore areas where they bump into their own duplicity. It may be trying to appear to be more than we are, trying to have more than we can afford, or trying to do more than we really can. Then, to take a courageous step in the direction of simplicity, focusing on God's purposes for you, trusting that your limits are OK.

That's simplicity. That's what leads to soul health.

*Mindy Caliguire serves in the area of spiritual formation at Willow Creek Community Church in South Barrington, Illinois. Visit her Web site at www.soulcare.com.*

# EPISODE 7 | OUR GOD

# Can God Live in Me?

## ENTER

"The world had changed."
—Opening line, *Lord of the Rings: The Fellowship of the Ring*, 2001

After Jesus ascended into Heaven, his followers obeyed his instructions. They waited. Christ had completed his time on earth. But the Holy Spirit was coming to dwell within the lives of Christ's followers. The world had changed. And it was about to change even more. Think about how you might be part of that change now.

> It's your turn to be on the crew of *Extreme Makeover: Home Edition*. Imagine you've just found out Jesus is coming to live in your house next week.
> - What room renovations would you tackle first?
> - What would you keep the same?
> - What would be the "special project" for you—something you'd want to redesign on your own and keep secret until the last minute?

"Christ has no body now but yours,
No hands, no feet on earth but yours,
Yours are the eyes through which
   he looks compassion on this world,
Christ has no body now on earth but yours."
—attributed to Teresa of Avila

### Consider it

"The love of God for his elect, having descended from on high and overcome every obstacle, has poured itself into the deep bed of our regenerated hearts. And to this he adds the grace of making the soul understand, drink, and taste of that love."
—Abraham Kuyper, *The Work of the Holy Spirit*, www.ccel.org

## DRINK

*In my former book, Theophilus, I wrote about all that Jesus began to do and to teach until the day he was taken up to heaven, after giving instructions through the Holy Spirit to the apostles he had chosen. After his suffering, he showed himself to these men and gave many convincing proofs that he was alive. He appeared to them over a period of forty days and spoke about the kingdom of God. On one occasion, while he was eating with them, he gave them this command: "Do not leave Jerusalem, but wait for the gift my Father promised, which you have heard me speak about. For John baptized with water, but in a few days you will be baptized with the Holy Spirit."*

*So when they met together, they asked him, "Lord, are you at this time going to restore the kingdom to Israel?"*

*He said to them: "It is not for you to know the times or dates the Father has set by his own authority. But you will receive power when the Holy Spirit comes on you; and you will be my witnesses in Jerusalem, and in all Judea and Samaria, and to the ends of the earth."*

—Acts 1:1-8

18 | FAITH CAFÉ

*When the day of Pentecost came, they were all together in one place. Suddenly a sound like the blowing of a violent wind came from heaven and filled the whole house where they were sitting. They saw what seemed to be tongues of fire that separated and came to rest on each of them. All of them were filled with the Holy Spirit and began to speak in other tongues as the Spirit enabled them.*

—Acts 2:1-4

## SAVOR

This story helps give an understanding of what God's Spirit is to Christ's followers.

Helen Keller's parents looked for a teacher who could work with their daughter. They found the perfect fit in a nineteen-year-old orphan, Anne Sullivan. She accepted the assignment of teaching Helen, who was six and had been unable to see, hear, or speak since she was nineteen months old. Anne entered Helen's life and changed it forever. Helen no longer had to try to find ways to live. She had a guide, a teacher, and a helper.

God knows we cannot obey him on our own. He sent the Guide, the Teacher, the Helper. His Spirit can enter our lives and change us forever.

Anne surely helped Helen. With a manual alphabet and hours of training, Helen soon learned to read and write in Braille. By the time she was ten, Helen learned sounds by placing her fingers on Anne's larynx and sensing the vibrations. Anne later spelled out lectures to Helen, who became a student at Radcliffe College. Speaker, author, and one who offered hope to those who were blind and deaf, Helen could not have done any of it without Anne's hand, her voice, and her help.

After Anne died in 1936, Helen wrote this about her friend: "My teacher is so near to me that I scarcely think of myself apart from her. I feel that her being is inseparable from my own, and that the footsteps of my life are in hers. All the best of me belongs to her; there is not a talent or an inspiration or a joy in me that has not been awakened by her loving touch."

(Van Morris, Mount Washington, Kentucky; source: *Helen Keller, The Story of My Life*)

## EXPERIENCE

As we seek to understand more about who the Holy Spirit is, the best place to start is in Scripture.

"But the Counselor, the Holy Spirit, whom the Father will send in my name, will teach you all things and will remind you of everything I have said to you."

—John 14:26, 27

### Look into it

- See texts on the Holy Spirit at www.ccel.org
- Russ Lee's site at www.russlee.com
- J. I. Packer, *Keep in Step with the Spirit*
- Billy Graham, *The Holy Spirit*

## WALK

If we believe God's Spirit has come to empower Christ's followers to be witnesses of his message, the world will change.

If you are a Christian, but have never consciously welcomed the Spirit to empower you, do that before seeking to follow any lists.

- Thank God daily for allowing his presence to live in your life.
- Make a list of ten ways your life will be different now that you celebrate God's presence in you.
- Welcome God's Spirit into your inner world. Think of one area of your thoughts or feelings that perhaps you have been reluctant to let God touch. Turn that area over to him in prayer.

**This week's spiritual discipline is waiting:**
This waiting isn't the same as putting things off. Waiting on God is a choice to remove our thoughts and actions from our usual distractions. Waiting can be a spiritual discipline when one sits alone near God—and waits. Maybe for something. Maybe for nothing. Schedule an appointment this week to find a good location and sit in stillness. The disciples waited for God's Spirit to invade. Not such a bad idea, is it?

**EPISODE 8 | OUR GOD**

# Can God Use Me?

## ENTER

As we think about how God can do something of value through our lives, let us listen to the advice of those who have gone before us. Paul the apostle knew about failure and wrong choices. He also knew about experiencing God's love, acceptance, and forgiveness. Let's read his words and receive this truth.

> Think of what would be on your Top Ten list of resolutions you have made for yourself. Take a moment to jot your list down.
> - How many of the items on your list are things you have worked at achieving?
> - How many of the items on your list are things you have invited God to work on in you?

### Consider it

"I believe God made me for a purpose, but he also made me fast. And when I run, I feel his pleasure."

—Eric Liddell, from *Chariots of Fire*

## DRINK

*Or didn't you realize that your body is a sacred place, the place of the Holy Spirit? Don't you see that you can't live however you please, squandering what God paid such a high price for? The physical part of you is not some piece of property belonging to the spiritual part of you.*

—1 Corinthians 6:19 *(The Message)*

*He used the apostles and prophets for the foundation. Now he's using you, fitting you in brick by brick, stone by stone, with Christ Jesus as the cornerstone that holds all the parts together. We see it taking shape day after day—a holy temple built by God.*

—Ephesians 2:20, 21 *(The Message)*

Paul wrote about doctrine and beliefs in his letters. He clearly stated truth about followers of Christ not living in isolation, but functioning as a corporate team, each part crucial for the whole. Since we've learned that God's Spirit can dwell in each of us, can we imagine seeing that Spirit teeming through all believers to fulfill God's goal to change the world?

## SAVOR

There are smells, and then, there are smells! I prefer some smells to others. Freshly baked bread, a pot roast cooking in the oven, scented candles, and a newly mowed lawn, just to name a few. Then there are those "other" smells. The ones we try to avoid, like garbage, sewage, annoyed skunks . . . you get the picture.

As my toddler approached me, I could tell he needed my assistance with one of those "other" smells. "Mommy," he said, sporting a coy expression, "could you change me?" I'll spare you any further adjectives regarding the transaction that followed. But I will share his response once I finished the job: "Thank you, Mommy. Thank you for changing me." This may come as a surprise, but during their toddler years, each of my children has thanked me for changing them! Thinking of their sincere appreciation still warms my heart.

20 | FAITH CAFÉ

My current toddler's gratitude brings a smile to my face. Like his older siblings, he realizes his predicament. Additionally, he knows that any attempt to remedy it on his own would only bring further mess. So he comes to me.

As humans, we can get ourselves into some pretty stinky situations. Sometimes, we take a wrong turn (or two) and end up stuck in a ditch on a less than desirable road. Our Father God watches and waits. Not wanting any to be misled, he pauses to hear our cry. "Uh, God, will you change me? I am so tired of being in this mess I have made. Please change me, God."

He does not turn his ear from that cry. No good father could. "I waited patiently for the LORD; he turned to me and heard my cry. He lifted me out of the slimy pit, out of the mud and mire; he set my feet on a rock and gave me a firm place to stand" (Psalm 40:1, 2).

Think over the times in your life when God has rescued you. Maybe you got into a wrong crowd, a wrong relationship or a wrong lifestyle. You called on God, and he lifted you out and set you down on a "firm place." Thank him for that. Thank him for changing you.

Or, maybe you find that you are still on that road. You're just not ready to give up that way of life. Just be honest with God. He'll meet you where you are. He knows the mess you're in (he smells it!). But he's waiting on you.

(Mary DeMent, "Giving Thanks," used by permission)

## EXPERIENCE

"The kind of work God usually calls you to is the kind of work (a) that you need most to do and (b) that the world most needs to have done. If you really get a kick out of work, you've presumably met requirements (a), but if your work is writing TV deodorant commercials, the chances are you've missed requirement (b). On the other hand, if your work is being a doctor in a leper colony, you have probably met requirement (b), but if most of the time you're bored and depressed by it, the chances are you have not only bypassed (a) but probably aren't helping your patients much either. . . . The place God calls you to is the place where your deep gladness and the world's deep hunger meet."

—Frederick Buechner,
*Wishful Thinking: A Theological ABC*

### Look into it
- Mindy Caliguire, *Discovering Soul Care*
- Larry Crabb, *Connecting: Healing Ourselves and Our Relationships*
- Rick Rusaw and Eric Swanson, *Living a Life on Loan*
- *Chariots of Fire*, Warner Home Video, 2005

## WALK

Choose this week to serve by making another Top Ten list—listing some of the "bricks" that need to be added or changed in you to become a "holy temple." God has called you for such a time as this!

"Be kind, for everyone you know is facing a great battle."

—Philo of Alexandria

Make sure your bricks are placed on a sure foundation and aren't just part of a facade.
- Stop pretending. Start doing.
- Stop lying. Speak the truth in love.
- Stop complaining. Start working at making things better.

**This week's spiritual discipline is accountability:** All followers of Christ are on the same team. None of us should do this alone. Accountability—helping one another walk through the journey correctly—is a vital part of this spiritual experience. Pursue a relationship with someone who won't gossip, but will offer advice and prayer or just listen to your goals. Try to meet and pray together twice this week. Don't expect perfection from the other person or yourself. Just be a friend who is honest.

## EPISODE 9 | OUR WORLD

# What Happens at Home?

## ENTER

After we tend to our packed schedules, come home for dinner, and pay our bills, what happens? How do we be the people God wants us to be at home?

Think of your childhood. Think of holidays, vacations, conversations, games, arguments, laughter, and hugs. Think of today.

- What words describe your family?
- Who are the members of your *real* family? Are you close to them?
- How well does your family know you? How well do you know them?

### Consider it
- 44% of adults say that having a satisfying family life is their highest priority in life.
- 18% of people said that completely understanding and carrying out the principles of their faith was the highest priority in their lives.

—from a 2005 Barna Research poll, www.barna.org

## DRINK

*Get rid of all bitterness, rage and anger, brawling and slander, along with every form of malice. Be kind and compassionate to one another, forgiving each other, just as in Christ God forgave you.*

—Ephesians 4:31, 32

*Submit to one another out of reverence for Christ. Wives, submit to your husbands as to the Lord. For the husband is the head of the wife as Christ is the head of the church, his body, of which he is the Savior. Now as the church submits to Christ, so also wives should submit to their husbands in everything.*

*Husbands, love your wives, just as Christ loved the church and gave himself up for her to make her holy, cleansing her by the washing with water through the word, and to present her to himself as a radiant church, without stain or wrinkle or any other blemish, but holy and blameless. In this same way, husbands ought to love their wives as their own bodies. He who loves his wife loves himself. After all, no one ever hated his own body, but he feeds and cares for it, just as Christ does the church—for we are members of his body.*

—Ephesians 5:21-30

## SAVOR

The kids secured their bike helmets and prepared to leave. It had been a great day at the park, but the clouds were closing in fast. I knew we needed to leave immediately if we intended to remain dry all the way home. The last thing I wanted was a brisk stroll in the rain with two preschoolers and an infant in tow. So I urged them to pick up the pace.

My oldest son led the way; I followed, pushing the baby in the stroller. And my three-year-old daughter was right behind us. At least I *thought* she was right behind us. I turned around and saw that she was lingering inside the park fence. I motioned for my oldest son to wait. Then I hurried back to gather my daughter. There she was, leisurely picking wild flowers. "Here, Mommy, I picked these for you," she said in her cute, little-girl voice.

22 | FAITH CAFÉ

Dark clouds hovered directly over our heads. Thunder sounded in the distance. A light drizzle began to fall. And my daughter was picking flowers. I shook my head and placed her firmly on her bike. "To obey is better than sacrifice!" I reprimanded.

As the verse left my lips, I understood it for the very first time.

On any other occasion, I would welcome my daughter's "sacrifice" of flowers. However, flowers were not what I needed at that moment.

She bypassed my instructions in order to please me. However, her plan failed. I was not pleased. Instead, I was angered. I couldn't fully appreciate her gift while concerned about her safety.

Sometimes we act like three-year-olds. We attempt to please God with our "sacrifices" and offerings. We reason that, if we do this or that, he will be delighted. We neglect his commands and carry on with our *own* game plan. God is not pleased. Saul feared man. Consequently, he chose to modify God's orders to his own liking. "But Samuel replied, 'Does the LORD delight in burnt offerings and sacrifices as much as in obeying the voice of the LORD? To obey is better than sacrifice, and to heed is better than the fat of rams. For rebellion is like the sin of divination, and arrogance like the evil of idolatry" (1 Samuel 15:22, 23). By circumventing God's plan, we are, in essence, like Saul, saying we know more than God. God desires obedience.

Is there a storm brewing in your life? Are you facing a major decision? Whatever your position, listen to that "still, small voice" of God. He wants to lead you safely Home.

(from Mary DeMent, "Heading Home," used by permission)

## EXPERIENCE

"According to Foster, submission does not demand self-hatred or loss of identity. Instead, it simply means growing secure in the conviction that 'our happiness is not dependent on getting what we want' but on the fulfillment that naturally flows from love of one's neighbors. Such wise and encouraging suggestions have helped many readers to discard the idea that discipline is an onerous duty and to move toward a liberating and simpler idea of discipline—whose defining character, as Foster never forgets, is joy."

—reviewer Michael Joseph Gross on Richard Foster's *Celebration of Discipline*

### Look into it
- William F. Harley, Jr., *His Needs, Her Needs*
- Dr. Kevin Leman, *Bringing Up Kids Without Tearing Them Down*
- Dr. Henry Cloud and Dr. John Townsend, *Boundaries*
- www.family.org
- www.familylife.com
- www.fln.org
- www.marriagebuilders.com/index.html
- www.fathersforlife.org/divorce/chldrndiv.htm

## WALK

Contact some of your relatives this week. Ask the Holy Spirit to direct your decisions about whom to write or call. Pray for each member of your family or close friends every day this week. Make steps toward forgiving family members who have hurt you, and accept God's forgiveness for your past mistakes.

If you have no family near you, view this list as advice for your close relationships.

- **Pray** as a family and pray separately.
- **Say** what should be said and remain silent when the words could bring damage.
- **Display** true Christian character at home.
- **Play** together and laugh; have fun and go to ball games, concerts, mountains, or beaches.
- **Stay** together by not giving up; be determined to endure, commit, and hope.

**This week's spiritual discipline is submission:** We often panic when we hear this word. However, its misuse does not give us a reason to ignore it. To whom will you submit this week? How can doing that inspire your relationship with God?

# EPISODE 10 | OUR WORLD

# What Happens at Work?

## ENTER

Whether you're a stay-at-home parent or a nine-to-five cubicle inhabitant, doing your job—doing it well and in a way that would please God—can be a challenge. How do we live the life God wants for us at work?

"When we set out to hear God's voice, we do not listen as though it will come from somewhere above us or in the room around us. It comes to us from *within*, in the heart, the dwelling place of God."
—John Eldredge, *Waking the Dead*

"I find that doing the will of God leaves me no time for disputing about his plans."
—George MacDonald

Describe a day in your work life.
- What time do you arrive at work?
- How far do you drive?
- What mood are you usually in before, during, and after work?
- What do you wear?
- How close are you to your coworkers?
- Is this what you dreamed of doing?

### Consider it
"If you don't have time to do it right, when will you have time to do it over?"
—John Wooden, former UCLA basketball coach

## DRINK

*Therefore, as God's chosen people, holy and dearly loved, clothe yourselves with compassion, kindness, humility, gentleness and patience. Bear with each other and forgive whatever grievances you may have against one another. Forgive as the Lord forgave you. And over all these virtues put on love, which binds them all together in perfect unity.*

*Let the peace of Christ rule in your hearts, since as members of one body you were called to peace. And be thankful. Let the word of Christ dwell in you richly as you teach and admonish one another with all wisdom, and as you sing psalms, hymns and spiritual songs with gratitude in your hearts to God. And whatever you do, whether in word or deed, do it all in the name of the Lord Jesus, giving thanks to God the Father through him.*
—Colossians 3:12-17

## SAVOR

When he finally arrives, blazing in beauty and all his angels with him, the Son of Man will take his place on his glorious throne. Then all the nations will be arranged before him and he will sort the people out, much as a shepherd sorts out sheep and goats, putting sheep to his right and goats to his left.

Then the King will say to those on his right, "Enter, you who are blessed by my Father! Take what's coming to you in this kingdom. It's been ready for you since the world's foundation. And here's why:
I was hungry and you fed me,
I was thirsty and you gave me a drink,
I was homeless and you gave me a room,
I was shivering and you gave me clothes,
I was sick and you stopped to visit,

24 | FAITH CAFÉ

I was in prison and you came to me."

Then those "sheep" are going to say, "Master, what are you talking about? When did we ever see you hungry and feed you, thirsty and give you a drink? And when did we ever see you sick or in prison and come to you?"

Then the King will say, "I'm telling the solemn truth: Whenever you did one of these things to someone overlooked or ignored, that was me—you did it to me."

Then he will turn to the goats, the ones on his left, and say, "Get out, worthless goats! You're good for nothing but the fires of hell. And why? Because—

I was hungry and you gave me no meal,
I was thirsty and you gave me no drink,
I was homeless and you gave me no bed,
I was shivering and you gave me no clothes,
Sick and in prison, and you never visited."

Then those "goats" are going to say, "Master, what are you talking about? When did we ever see you hungry or thirsty or homeless or shivering or sick or in prison and didn't help?"

He will answer them, "I'm telling the solemn truth: Whenever you failed to do one of these things to someone who was being overlooked or ignored, that was me—you failed to do it to me."

Then those "goats" will be herded to their eternal doom, but the "sheep" to their eternal reward.

—Matthew 25:31-46 (*The Message*)

## EXPERIENCE

"Be very careful, then, how you live—not as unwise but as wise, making the most of every opportunity, because the days are evil. Therefore do not be foolish, but understand what the Lord's will is."

—Ephesians 5:15-17

Whether at home, in the fields, in an office, or on a turnpike, you have the opportunity each day to live like Jesus and show his light to those around you. Don't miss it! Find resources that help you make the most of your working hours.

### Look into it

- www.leaderslighthouse.com
- www.christianadvice.net/christianity_at_work.htm
- www.christiansatwork.org.uk/cgi-bin/caw.cgi
- www.christatwork.org/templates/System/details.asp?id=22809&PID=64231
- Rob Briner, *Roaring Lambs*
- Mark Greene, *Thank God It's Monday*

## WALK

Acts of service can remind us of what God did for us. Didn't Jesus say that whatever we do for others is what we actually do for him? Seek ways to serve Jesus in this coming work week.

Take some time at the beginning of your work day to talk to God: *Father, you have placed me in this position. Forgive me for missing so many opportunities to make a positive difference. Speak through me and love through me. Make my world better as you work through me at work. In Jesus' name, Amen.*

As a group, find a few ministries in your area which offer services to those in need, and plan to work on a project together. Get involved. Challenge and be challenged.

- Serve food to the hungry.
- Plan a clothing drive.
- Visit people in a nursing home.

**This week's spiritual discipline is service:** Service is often viewed as a duty rather than a spiritual discipline. Jesus set a much different example. He gave and cared. He looked for ways to prove his love for others. Think about how people have helped you and served you. Come up with wild ideas for "doing good unto others" at work. Be willing to serve in ways you've never served before. Serve by doing, even when no one will know who served.

## EPISODE 11 | OUR WORLD

# What Happens at Church?

## ENTER

"Life occurs between people as well as within them."
—Nathan Schwartz-Salant, *The Mystery of Human Relationship*

"Let us not give up meeting together, as some are in the habit of doing, but let us encourage one another."
—Hebrews 10:25

What about the people sitting beside you? Do you know them? Do they know you?

Think about what might happen if we worked together to apply our spiritual principles in a corporate body of true friends—not just those who sometimes act like friends, but those who choose to become friends because of sharing forgiveness and redemption by the same blood.

Let's think about our church experience.
- Make a list of some things you don't like about church.
- Make a list of things you do like about church.
- What lessons do you think God is trying to teach you through your church experience?
- How should you respond to the challenges you face so God is honored?
- In what ways can you help to make Christ's body where you are alive, active, and growing?

### Consider it
"People go to church for the same reasons they go to a tavern: to stupefy themselves, to forget their misery, to imagine themselves, for a few minutes anyway, free and happy."
—Mikhail Bakunin, Russian philosopher

## DRINK

*Just as each of us has one body with many members, and these members do not all have the same function, so in Christ we who are many form one body, and each member belongs to all the others. We have different gifts, according to the grace given us. If a man's gift is prophesying, let him use it in proportion to his faith. If it is serving, let him serve; if it is teaching, let him teach; if it is encouraging, let him encourage; if it is contributing to the needs of others, let him give generously; if it is leadership, let him govern diligently; if it is showing mercy, let him do it cheerfully.*
—Romans 12:4-8

Paul wrote to a group of leaders who struggled to agree. Grace, rules, methods of worship, who does what—all are issues with which today's church is still grappling. Here Paul chose to highlight the variety of gifts while stressing the importance of teamwork. We need to remember to do that today.

## SAVOR

As my obstetrician warned me about the baby's place, I feared the birth of our next child. We did not have insurance, and the cost of complicated work would be a lot. As the doctor expressed risks associated with

26 | FAITH CAFÉ

our options, comfort did not come to me. I wasn't sure what to do next.

Of course, I asked people to pray. But did I really mean it? Believe in it? Pray myself? Or is "pray for me" just something I tend to say in times of unrest? While these questions circled my already disoriented brain, a handful of women expressed their urge to intercede for me. Each mentioned that thoughts of my unborn child's positioning woke them up in the middle of the night and prompted them to prayer. Thank God! One felt led to gather together, pray and lay hands on me, as instructed in James 5:14. At least one felt led to fast and did so on my behalf. Another stopped praying and began thanking God for the work she knew he would do. Wow! So, knowing that, I walked into my next doctor's appointment confident that the baby had turned, right? Wrong.

Besides the doctor, no one was more surprised when the doctor said, "Well, the head is down. The baby turned." I lay there frozen. What? "It must have been all of those prayers," he said smiling. Then his face turned serious. "I have to admit," he said, "I did not think this baby was going to turn."

Prayer. I've read several books on the subject. I observe it. And I can pinpoint countless references in Scripture urging us to practice it. Still, sometimes, I just do not understand how it works. Is that really necessary, though? As I think about it, there are several technological items I use but fail to totally grasp their inner workings. My failure to fully understand does not prevent me from embracing them on a daily basis.

What is going on in your life? Is there something you desire God to turn around? Maybe it's a disobedient child or a distant spouse. Maybe it's a job or financial situation. I do not know your need. But I do know that God is able to turn lives in a different direction. Just as he literally turned my son around in my womb, he is more than able to turn your life, your circumstances around. Though you and I may not totally comprehend it, he uses the avenue of prayer, our conversations with him, to accomplish that goal. And he likes it when we invite others into our lives to join us in prayer.

(Mary DeMent, "Turning Point Prayers," used by permission)

## EXPERIENCE

"Ninety-eight percent of U.S. churches have fewer than 300 in attendance on any Sunday morning; 85 percent of these experience a net loss or no net gain in membership each year; 2,000 new churches are started each year; 6,000 are closed permanently."

—Sweet, McLaren, and Haselmayer, *A Is for Abductive: The Language of the Emerging Church*

### Look into it
- www.adherents.com/rel_USA.html
- Calvin Miller, *O Shepherd, Where Art Thou?*
- Rick Warren, *The Purpose Driven Church*

## WALK

How can your group make your local church even better? Be creative and think out loud of things that this smaller body can do, not by demanding that things be changed in a certain way, but by loving people, praying, caring, serving, and using spiritual gifts to make a huge difference.

Some ideas:
- Send a card to or visit a church member who is sick. Decide to make this a regular activity.
- Volunteer to greet people at the next service.
- Think of a talent or gift that you have, and name one way this could be used to serve the church.

**This week's spiritual discipline is celebration:** Celebration is not about just doing what we like to do. Spiritual celebration is choosing to rejoice because of God—not only for what he has done for us, but more for who he is. It involves praise and worship, reverence and awe, excitement and intimacy.

Choose to celebrate God in various settings this week. As you celebrate, make sure you do not let what you like or dislike about worship styles get in the way of you and God. God wants you to honor him. So do it.

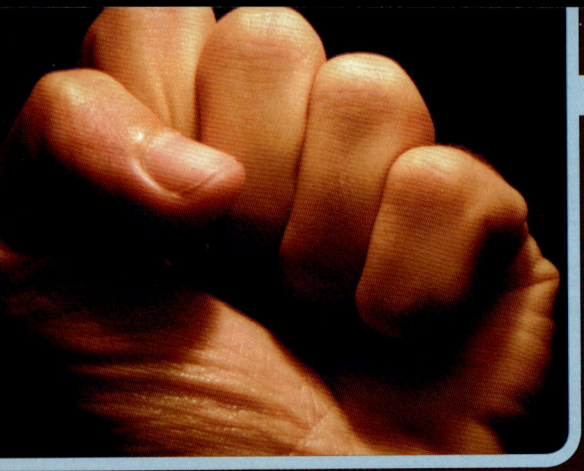

# EPISODE 12 | OUR WORLD

# What Happens with My Enemies?

## ENTER

We've talked about family and church and careers. We've learned about God's will for our relationships with siblings, coworkers, and church members. But what about those we hate? What about those who hate us? What about nations we are now at war against?

We don't have to love them, do we? *Do we?*

---

Let's plan a strategy for attack. The first step is to identify our enemies.

- Who do you see as enemies of our country? of Christians? of your own family?
- Why are these groups or persons considered enemies?
- What could be done to change your view of them as enemies?

---

### Consider it

"Father, forgive them; they don't know what they're doing."

—Luke 23:34 (*The Message*)

## DRINK

*When a Samaritan woman came to draw water, Jesus said to her, "Will you give me a drink?" (His disciples had gone into the town to buy food.)*

*The Samaritan woman said to him, "You are a Jew and I am a Samaritan woman. How can you ask me for a drink?" (For Jews do not associate with Samaritans.)*

—John 4:7-9

"You have an enemy. He is trying to steal your freedom, kill your heart, destroy your life."

—John Eldredge, *Waking the Dead*

The hostility between Jews and Samarians had developed centuries before this moment when Jesus stopped at the well. The customs and religious practices of the Samaritans were different from the Jews, and the Jews considered this people to be a mixed race and inferior to them. They did not associate with the Samaritans at all, if they could help it. In fact, rather than using the shortest route from Judea to Galilee, which went through Samaria, the Jews would make a long detour around the area. But Jesus was different. He led his disciples straight through, no doubt revealing more to them than just a short cut.

We must realize that the people we struggle to like are not the real enemy. The Bible teaches that Satan is our foe. People, even those who act in hateful ways, are loved by God. This session is designed to help us remember the identity of our true foe and choose to display Christ's character to those around us. Even the ones we may dislike we can choose to treat with honor.

## SAVOR

My friend and I browsed through a bookstore. I struck up a conversation with the store manager. He seemed friendly and eager to know more about us. Halfway through our conversation I told him we were both pastors.

He was shocked. Not because he doesn't like ministers, but because he'd never really had a decent conversation with a Christian. "I normally only hear from Christians when they are mad," he told us.

28 | FAITH CAFÉ

The three of us sat down at the coffee bar. The manager told tales about religious people who had called, written or walked in his store to inform him they would never do business with him because of objectionable books or Halloween displays.

The man thanked us for being different and then excused himself so he could get back to work. My thoughts were racing so fast I found it hard to finish my bagel. No bestseller could have taught us what we learned from that honest man.

I asked my friend, and myself, "How can believers shine a light and promote the gospel in a sinful, wicked world?" Maybe God wants people today to follow the example of Jesus. Time and technology have changed, but yesterday's techniques can still touch today's world.

Sitting idly as silent witnesses isn't enough. Lumbering ahead to peddle words without the Spirit is too much. We need to reach the world as Jesus did. He models a personal, realistic approach to speaking forth the good news. Let's stare at him again. Let's discover the steps Christ used to initiate conversation with the people he met, and open the door for true evangelism.

(Chris Maxwell, *Beggars Can Be Chosen*)

## EXPERIENCE

"The greatness of a man cannot be seen in the hours of comfort and convenience, but rather in the moments of conflict and adversity."
—Dr. Martin Luther King Jr.

What does it mean to forgive the enemies who seek to destroy us? As you watch, read, or listen to the news this week, think about what forgiveness could look like.

### Look into it
- www.scu.edu/ethics/publications/ethicalperspectives/spohn.html
- Hal Donaldson, *Midnight in the City*
- John Ortberg, *The Life You've Always Wanted*

## WALK

"Reading the daily paper can, in conjunction with journaling, be a conscious time of prayer for the world. We may write of our concern for earthquake victims, our fear of nuclear disaster, our joy at a new birth or a peace accord. As we journal in response to the daily news, we interact with what is happening in the world; we feel more strongly the connections between ourselves and others around the globe."
—Anne Broyles, *Journaling: A Spiritual Journey*

As you read the news this week, think of Jesus' response to his enemies. Jesus broke rules by hanging out with those his custom told him to avoid. But he loved them and loves us too much to play a political game. All people are those Christ loves. All people are those for whom Christ died.

Commit to a strategy for dealing with your enemies this week—not out of hatred, but out of love.

- Write letters of kindness, encouragement, or forgiveness.
- When you talk and disagree with someone, consciously decide to end the conversations with love.
- Watch the news at least one night. See those toward whom you and your country feel hatred. Choose to intercede for those your nation fights against. Pray, asking God to remind them of his love.

**This week's spiritual discipline is confession:** Who have you wronged? Who have you hated? It is time to ask for forgiveness. Do not justify your behavior or rationalize any reasons for its occurrence. Read this prayer aloud: "Forgive us our debts, as we also have forgiven our debtors" (Matthew 6:12).

Now tell God you are sorry. Ask him to forgive you and to help you not to act badly toward others.

Receive his forgiveness.

And, for those times when the others know you have wronged them, confess to them and ask to be forgiven.

# EPISODE 13 | OUR WORLD

# How Far Does This Go?

## ENTER

"I ran and ran and ran every day, and I acquired this sense of determination, this sense of spirit that I would never, never give up, no matter what happened."
—Wilma Rudolph, runner, U.S. gold medalist in 1960 Olympics

How do we respond to that urge to which Wilma Rudolph referred? Our life shouldn't be all about achieving our own accomplishments. But neither is life about just knowing biblical truth. The reality of our beliefs comes out in how we run the race. And the true spiritual victory comes as we serve others.

How do we—how can we—run toward a spiritual victory every day? Think about these questions.

- What do I need to leave behind in order to run most effectively?
- How can I be sure my path is straight?
- Where do I believe God wants me to go?

### Consider it

"If the fields are white for harvest, why do we spend all our money on painting the barn?"
—C. Thomas Davis, *Fields of the Fatherless*

## DRINK

"If anyone would come after me, he must deny himself and take up his cross and follow me. For whoever wants to save his life will lose it, but whoever loses his life for me will find it."
—Matthew 16:24, 25

We are God's workmanship, created in Christ Jesus to do good works, which God prepared in advance for us to do.
—Ephesians 2:10

He said to them, "Go into all the world and preach the good news to all creation."
—Mark 16:15

"Peter replied, 'Repent and be baptized, every one of you, in the name of Jesus Christ for the forgiveness of your sins. And you will receive the gift of the Holy Spirit. The promise is for you and your children and for all who are far off—for all whom the Lord our God will call.'"
—Acts 2:38, 39

## SAVOR

Fran traveled to Guatemala and displayed acts of kindness to poor people who have never heard the gospel. Jim flew to Mexico to help a mission organization build church auditoriums. Michael drove to New Orleans to repair damage from Hurricane Katrina. Marsha knows that her role as a hospital nurse is about much more than the medical condition of her patients or the policies and procedures of her staff; she views each day as a ministry opportunity. Karen

30 | FAITH CAFÉ

was not hired by a local congregation for a full-time ministry position, but she found a job and spends as much time as possible helping to encourage children and ladies in a church setting. Richard left his well-paying job to take on a ministry; he and his family serve breakfast and lunch to street people and hookers five days a week. Marvin knew God had bigger plans for him than his high-paying career and his status in the financial market; he chose to care for people that everyone seemed to ignore.

Each of those followers of Christ took their beliefs seriously. They lived them. They displayed the doctrine by actions. Outside of church auditoriums, in schools, in hospitals, on foreign land, and in nearby homeless shelters, the possibilities for influencing the world are many. Our lesson's question is legitimate: How far does this go? The answer, if we hold to biblical strategies, is this: *to the ends of the earth*. But the answer—since we are now the ones called by God to live and voice his love to others—is really this: *as far as we will take it*.

The gospel will go as far as we can go. That doesn't mean the same thing for all of us. Each one is called to use his or her gifts and experience to display God's truth to those needing it. Rather than just sermons and corrections, instead of formalities and formulas, let's all choose to voice the gospel in acts of kindness locally and globally. Start nearby. Be willing to travel to foreign soil if directed by God. But wherever God leads, find joy in the task of fulfilling the Great Commission.

## EXPERIENCE

There are all kinds of ways to support the spreading of the gospel, even without leaving your house. As you read and look at the resources listed below, think about how each ministry displays what all of us should seek to do in some way. Speaking truth in the language of every tribe. Reaching those who are not yet reached. Showing videos and telling stories to bring truth to people. Traveling to other countries. Learning how to think *locally* and *globally*. Realizing that those with disabilities are in desperate need of our message of truth.

### Look into it
- http://ccci.org
- http://www.ywam.org
- http://wycliffe.org
- http://tcci.org
- http://nathanielshope.org/
- Bob Briner, *Roaring Lambs*
- Elisabeth Elliot, *Through Gates of Splendor*
- Patrick Johnstone, *Operation World: When We Pray God Works*
- C. Thomas Davis, *Fields of the Fatherless*
- John Piper, *Don't Waste Your Life*

## WALK

"Simple acts of kindness are all it takes to change a life, a community, even a nation."
—C. Thomas Davis, *Fields of the Fatherless*

At work, at home, at the store: choose to notice those around you. Do not judge them or look down on them. Realize God has called you to shine his light of love to them. Allow his reflection to shine.

Consider ways your group could be involved in short-term missions.
- Financial support
- Prayer partnering
- Communicating with missionaries
- Planning or going on trips
- Telling the gospel message

**This week's spiritual discipline is journeying:** Journeying means going somewhere, meeting someone, or doing something we rarely do, with the single motive of showing God's love to someone else. Take time this week to travel down streets you normally ignore. Get to know someone new. Through your journey you may take the truth farther than you ever have.

# Daily Bible Readings

EPISODE 1: **How Do I See Myself?**
Day 1: Psalm 25:15-17
Day 2: Galatians 5:18-20
Day 3: John 16:17-22
Day 4: Ezra 9:4-6
Day 5: Colossians 3
Day 6: Psalm 8

EPISODE 2: **Who Am I Really?**
Day 1: John 1:1-13
Day 2: 1 John 3:1-10
Day 3: Galatians 2:4, 5; Galatians 5:1
Day 4: Romans 8:28-39
Day 5: 1 Corinthians 5:11-21
Day 6: Psalm 139

EPISODE 3: **Who Can I Become?**
Day 1: Psalm 52
Day 2: Ephesians 1
Day 3: Ephesians 2
Day 4: 1 Timothy 1:12-20
Day 5: Psalm 138
Day 6: Romans 12

EPISODE 4: **How Do I See God?**
Day 1: Job 3
Day 2: John 14
Day 3: Matthew 12
Day 4: John 10:11-18
Day 5: Matthew 26:36-39
Day 6: Matthew 11:28-30

EPISODE 5: **Is God My Father?**
Day 1: Nehemiah 9:16, 17
Day 2: Joel 3:16
Day 3: Deuteronomy 32:1-4
Day 4: 2 Corinthians 1:3-7
Day 5: Psalm 18
Day 6: Matthew 6:9-13

EPISODE 6: **What Did Jesus Do for Me?**
Day 1: Matthew 27:11-66
Day 2: Luke 24
Day 3: 1 Peter 3:18-22
Day 4: Galatians 4:4-7
Day 5: Romans 6:1-14
Day 6: Hebrews 10:1-10

EPIDSODE 7: **Can God Live in Me?**
Day 1: Acts 1
Day 2: Acts 2
Day 3: 2 Timothy 1:13, 14
Day 4: Galatians 5:16-26
Day 5: Psalm 51:6-12
Day 6: 1 John 4:12-16

EPISODE 8: **Can God Use Me?**
Day 1: Ephesians 2:19-22
Day 2: Matthew 28:16-20
Day 3: 1 Corinthians 3:8, 9
Day 4: 1 Corinthians 12
Day 5: 1 Corinthians 14
Day 6: 2 Corinthians 12:7-10

EPISODE 9: **What Happens at Home?**
Day 1: Joshua 24:15
Day 2: Titus 2:1-8
Day 3: 1 Peter 3:1-7
Day 4: Proverbs 4:3, 4
Day 5: Colossians 3:18-25
Day 6: Ephesians 6:1-4

EPISODE 10: **What Happens at Work?**
Day 1: 1 Thessalonians 5:12-18
Day 2: Philippians 2
Day 3: Matthew 5:13-16
Day 4: Proverbs 21
Day 5: Judges 6:11-16
Day 6: Proverbs 31

EPISODE 11: **What Happens at Church?**
Day 1: Matthew 16:13-20
Day 2: Acts 11:19-26
Day 3: Romans 16
Day 4: 1 Timothy 3
Day 5: 1 Peter 5
Day 6: 1 Corinthians 1:1-17

EPISODE 12: **What Happens with My Enemies?**
Day 1: Matthew 5:1-12
Day 2: Matthew 5:21-26, 38-48
Day 3: Proverbs 16:7
Day 4: Genesis 33
Day 5: 1 Samuel 24
Day 6: Psalm 143

EPISODE 13: **How Far Does This Go?**
Day 1: 2 Corinthians 3
Day 2: Psalm 18:46-50
Day 3: Acts 8:26-40
Day 4: Acts 10
Day 5: Psalm 96
Day 6: John 3:16, 17